SPOT and GUS

VOLCANO ADVENTURE

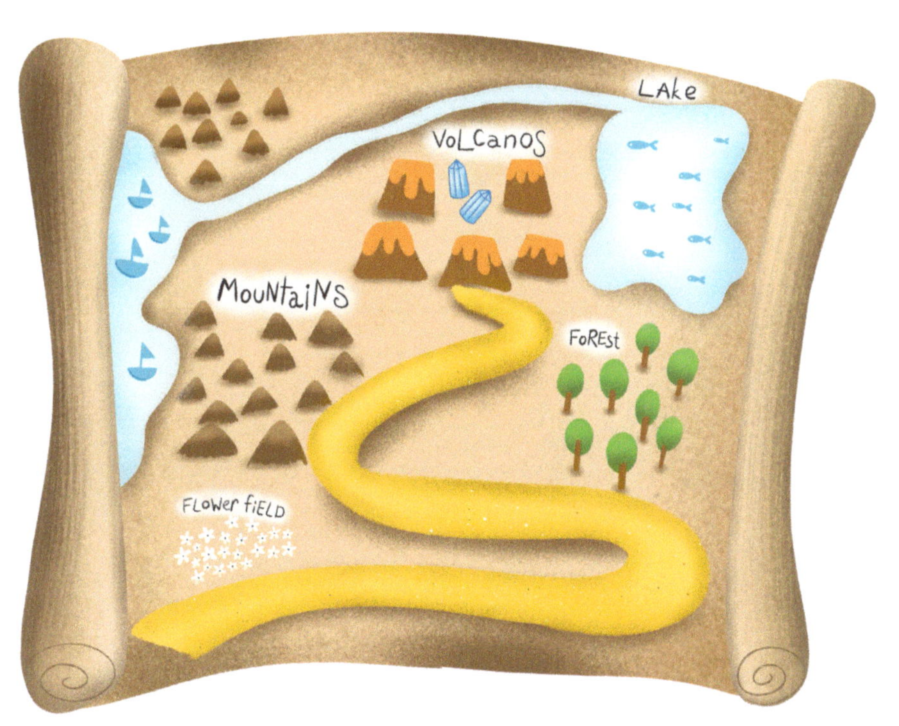
LAke
VoLCanoS
MOUNTaiNS
FoREst
FLOWeR fiELD

There once lived three best friends: Spot, the blue Diplo - docus, Gus, the yellow Stegosaurus and Archie, the purple Triceratrops. Their favourite thing in the world was to play together, they played all the time!

But one day Archie got sick, and couldn't play with his friends anymore.

"Archie, get well soon, we miss you" said Spot.
Archie couldn't answer, his temperature was very high.
Spot & Gus tried to give him fruit tea, keep him warm
and took care of Archie every possible way,
but no success. Archie's temperature was
still very hight.

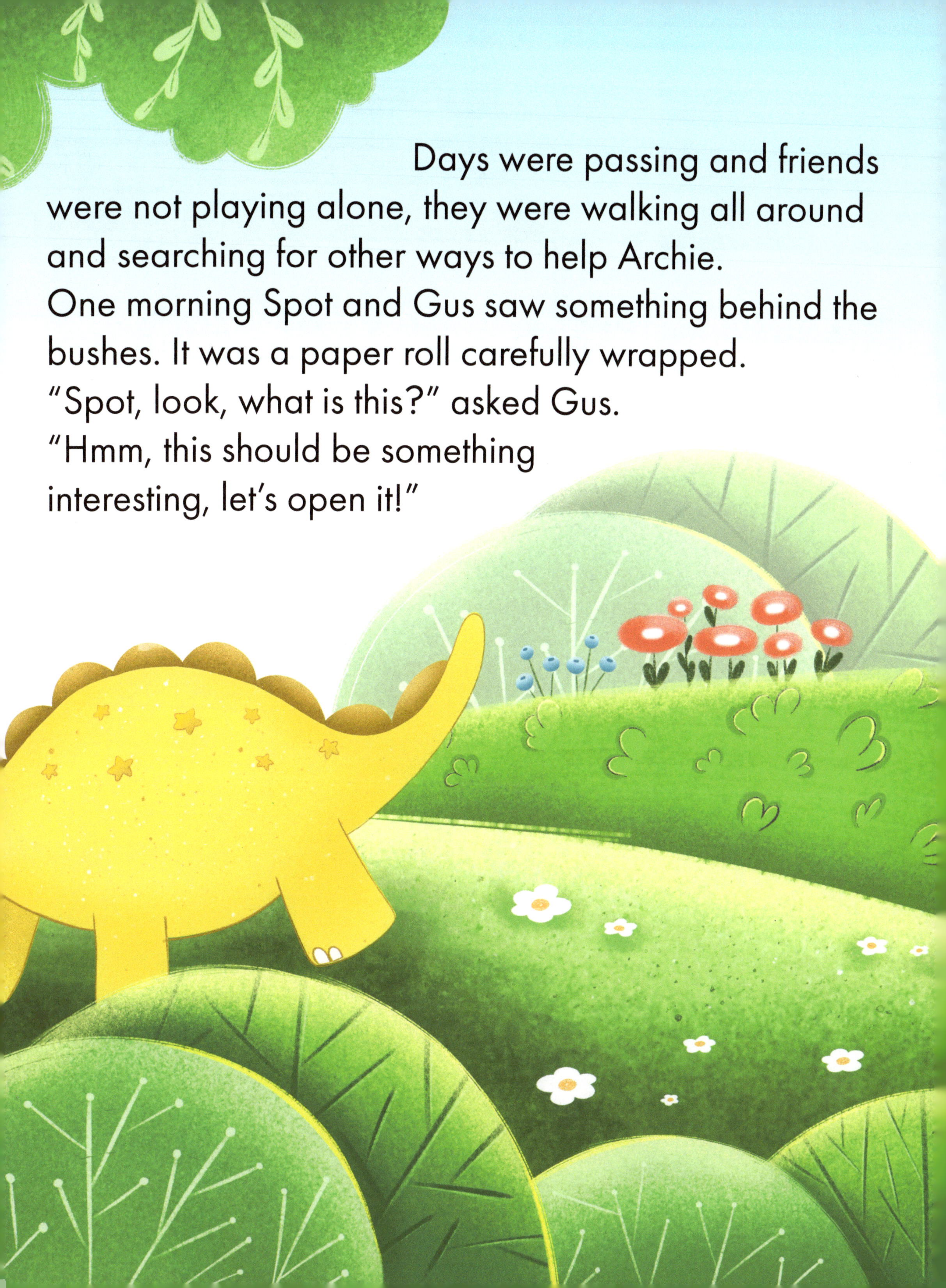

Days were passing and friends were not playing alone, they were walking all around and searching for other ways to help Archie.
One morning Spot and Gus saw something behind the bushes. It was a paper roll carefully wrapped.
"Spot, look, what is this?" asked Gus.
"Hmm, this should be something interesting, let's open it!"

VoLCaNoS
MouNTaiNS
FoRES
FLoWeR FiELD
<<In the very heart of volcano world there are magic crystals, and their magic is in the following:
If a sick person will touch a crystal, he will recover IMMEDIATELY! >>

Four hands carefully unwrapped the roll and exclaimed:
"It's a map!!" 
Their curious eyes observed the paper.
"Stones, mountains, volcanos, rivers...
what is written here, Spot?"
Spot was the eldest of three friends, and
he could already read.

<<In the very heart of volcano
world there are magic crystals,
and their magic is in the following:
If a sick person will touch a
crystal, he will recover
IMMEDIATELY! >>

"We can help Archie!" both friends
shouted at the same time "let's go, Gus, we need
to find crystals and bring them to Archie!"

Without even saying goodbye, Spot and Gus started their journey to volcanos, that were far away behind the mountains.

Far or near, Spot and Gus noticed a huge entrance and
an interesting stone creature looking at them.
"Hello! What are you searching for here?"
The stone creature's name was Rock-Rock. Spot and Gus
told him about their friend and the crystals.
"Yes, I know where to find them, follow me"
             said Rock-Rock and showed them the road
                that was taking to the heart of volcanos.

"Everybody calls me Wikipedia, I know everything!
Even more about the volcanos! Did you know,
that volcanos are mountains that erupt and
release hot lava, ash and gases?
Did you know that?

They are formed,   when magma from beneath the
Earth's surface breaks   through the crust. Volcanos can
be found on land and even underwater! Some of them
are sleeping, which means they are not currently erupting
but could do in the future!"

"Wow! And how the crystals appear here?" asked Gus.
He was astonished by Rock-Rock's story about
volcanos.
"Oh, that's my favorite part, when
volcano erupts,

the lava cools down and solidifies to form crystals in many shapes, sizes and colors, can you imagine?"
"Yes, yes, I've read about it, crystals like quartz, amethyst, obsidian..." said Spot.
"Exactly! Come friends, we are almost there!"

Spot and Gus noticed a dark
mountain with shining crater,
and a sparkling bee flying over it.
"Hi Rock-Rock, who is
with you?" A fairy volcano
bee looked curiously
at Spot and Gus.

Her name was Busy, she was collecting crystals and adding magic to them, so they would not only decorate Nature, but also help and cure sick animals.
"We are here for our friend, Archie. He got sick, and we need crystals to help him, can we borrow some, please?"

"I'm sorry for your friend, of course, I've added magic to those already, you can have it."
"Thank you, Busy!" Spot and Gus were so happy to find crystals. They wanted to go back as soon as possible, but suddenly...

They heard a very loud noise, coming from very near.
"Is it a thunder?" they looked at the sky, but it was clear.

B

"Eruption! Volcano is erupting!!!" screamed Rock-Rock, "we should run!"
Everybody was so surprised that just run where their eyes were.
"Gus...Gus! Where is Gus?"suddenly asked Spot.
They looked around and exhaled. Hot lava coming from volcano poured down and separated friends. Gus was on the other side of lava river. "We must do something! How can we help him?" Spot was very worried for his friend.
OM!

"I have an idea, quick, bring all the crystals here, and anything you can find, ropes, branches, everything!"

It suddenly hit them all at the same time: "A bridge!!!"

A bridge!!!

They immediately started collecting everything they could see around, even stones, to build a quick bridge, and when it was ready, Busy flew, moved the end to the other side and fixed the bridge with branches. "It's ready! Come, Gus, quickly, you can pass the bridge now!"

It was such a joy
to be reunited.

"Thank you for helping me,
friends, only.. now we have one
crystal remaining. We need to.."
He didn't finish speaking, when he saw the
last crystal flowing away with lava.

"Oh, no, the crystal..."
The last crystal was already swallowed by lava.

The day was coming to the night, and Spot and
Gus had to go home. They left Rock-Rock and Busy in
volcano world and went back home, tired and sad...
"Archie!!! Look, Spot, it's Archie! He is well!"
"Spot, Gus! Where have you been?" Archie was happy
to see his friends.
"We... crystals... volcanos..."friends couldn't believe
their eyes, "we thougt only magic crystals

would help you,
but we couldn't bring even
a single crystal" sadly answered Spot.

"Oh Spot, Gus! It's ok, I don't need magic crystals, **I already have one!**"

"Really? Where is it? How did you find it?"

"I didn't search for it. It was always here, with us! It's you and Gus! My mama says, that having friends who care about you is the purest and magical crystal in the whole world!"

To the reader

As we reach the end of this adventure with our dinosaurs, I'm filled with gratitude. Thank you for joining us on this journey. Writing and illustrating this book with my mom has been a joy, and knowing it's now in your hands is truly special.

I hope our first story brought you joy, and I go to write and illustrate the next magical story. More adventures are yet to come!

With warm regards,
Armine